50 Chinese Takeout Recipes Made at Home

By: Kelly Johnson

Table of Contents

- General Tso's Chicken
- Orange Chicken
- Sesame Chicken
- Sweet and Sour Chicken
- Kung Pao Chicken
- Mongolian Beef
- Beef and Broccoli
- Pepper Steak
- Honey Walnut Shrimp
- Salt and Pepper Shrimp
- Szechuan Shrimp
- Hot and Sour Soup
- Egg Drop Soup
- Wonton Soup
- Chicken Lo Mein
- Beef Lo Mein
- Shrimp Lo Mein
- Chicken Chow Mein
- Beef Chow Fun
- Shrimp Fried Rice
- Chicken Fried Rice
- Yangzhou Fried Rice
- Egg Foo Young
- Moo Goo Gai Pan
- Hunan Chicken
- Szechuan Chicken
- Cashew Chicken
- Lemon Chicken
- Crispy Duck with Hoisin Sauce
- Chinese BBQ Pork (Char Siu)
- Teriyaki Chicken
- Garlic Green Beans
- Mapo Tofu
- Salt and Pepper Tofu
- Steamed Fish with Ginger and Scallions

- Chinese Scallion Pancakes
- Spring Rolls
- Egg Rolls
- Crab Rangoon
- Dumplings (Jiaozi)
- Baozi (Steamed Pork Buns)
- Dan Dan Noodles
- Chinese Hot Pot
- Peking Duck
- Black Bean Chicken
- Cumin Lamb Stir-Fry
- Sichuan Dry-Fried Green Beans
- Hot and Spicy Tofu Stir-Fry
- Chinese Donuts (Youtiao)
- Red Bean Sesame Balls (Jian Dui)

General Tso's Chicken

Ingredients:

For the chicken:

- 1 lb (450g) boneless chicken thighs, cut into cubes
- ½ cup (65g) cornstarch
- 1 egg, beaten
- ½ teaspoon salt
- Oil for frying

For the sauce:

- 2 tablespoons soy sauce
- 1 tablespoon hoisin sauce
- 1 tablespoon rice vinegar
- 1 tablespoon sugar
- ½ teaspoon red chili flakes
- 1 teaspoon cornstarch mixed with 2 tablespoons water
- 2 cloves garlic, minced
- 1 teaspoon ginger, minced

Instructions:

1. Coat chicken in egg and cornstarch, then fry until golden.
2. Sauté garlic, ginger, and chili flakes.
3. Add sauce ingredients, then cornstarch slurry. Simmer until thick.
4. Toss chicken in the sauce and serve with rice.

Orange Chicken

Ingredients:

- 1 lb (450g) boneless chicken breast, cut into cubes
- ½ cup (65g) cornstarch
- 1 egg, beaten
- ½ teaspoon salt
- Oil for frying

For the sauce:

- ½ cup (120ml) orange juice
- 2 tablespoons soy sauce
- 1 tablespoon rice vinegar
- 2 tablespoons sugar
- 1 teaspoon orange zest
- 1 teaspoon cornstarch mixed with 2 tablespoons water
- 1 clove garlic, minced

Instructions:

1. Coat chicken in egg and cornstarch, then fry until crispy.
2. Sauté garlic, then add sauce ingredients and simmer.
3. Stir in cornstarch slurry and cook until thick.
4. Toss fried chicken in the sauce and serve.

Sesame Chicken

Ingredients:

- 1 lb (450g) boneless chicken, cut into cubes
- ½ cup (65g) cornstarch
- 1 egg, beaten
- ½ teaspoon salt
- Oil for frying

For the sauce:

- ¼ cup (60ml) soy sauce
- 2 tablespoons honey
- 1 tablespoon rice vinegar
- 1 teaspoon sesame oil
- 1 teaspoon cornstarch mixed with 2 tablespoons water
- 1 tablespoon toasted sesame seeds

Instructions:

1. Fry battered chicken until crispy.
2. Heat sauce ingredients in a pan until thickened.
3. Toss chicken in sauce and garnish with sesame seeds.

Sweet and Sour Chicken

Ingredients:

- 1 lb (450g) boneless chicken, cut into cubes
- ½ cup (65g) cornstarch
- 1 egg, beaten
- ½ teaspoon salt
- Oil for frying

For the sauce:

- ¼ cup (60ml) ketchup
- 2 tablespoons rice vinegar
- 2 tablespoons sugar
- 1 tablespoon soy sauce
- 1 teaspoon cornstarch mixed with 2 tablespoons water
- ½ cup (75g) pineapple chunks
- ½ cup (75g) bell peppers, chopped

Instructions:

1. Fry battered chicken until crispy.
2. Sauté bell peppers and pineapple, add sauce ingredients, and simmer.
3. Stir in cornstarch slurry until thick.
4. Toss chicken in sauce and serve.

Kung Pao Chicken

Ingredients:

- 1 lb (450g) boneless chicken, diced
- ¼ cup (30g) peanuts
- 2 dried red chilies, chopped
- 1 teaspoon ginger, minced
- 2 cloves garlic, minced
- ½ cup (75g) bell peppers, chopped

For the sauce:

- 2 tablespoons soy sauce
- 1 tablespoon rice vinegar
- 1 tablespoon sugar
- 1 teaspoon cornstarch mixed with 2 tablespoons water

Instructions:

1. Stir-fry chicken until cooked, then remove.
2. Sauté chilies, ginger, and garlic.
3. Add chicken, bell peppers, peanuts, and sauce.
4. Stir-fry until thickened.

Mongolian Beef

Ingredients:

- 1 lb (450g) flank steak, sliced thinly
- ¼ cup (30g) cornstarch
- Oil for frying

For the sauce:

- ¼ cup (60ml) soy sauce
- 2 tablespoons brown sugar
- 1 teaspoon ginger, minced
- 2 cloves garlic, minced
- 1 teaspoon cornstarch mixed with 2 tablespoons water

Instructions:

1. Coat beef in cornstarch and fry until crispy.
2. Sauté garlic and ginger, then add sauce ingredients.
3. Stir in cornstarch slurry and cook until thick.
4. Toss beef in the sauce and serve.

Beef and Broccoli

Ingredients:

- 1 lb (450g) flank steak, sliced thinly
- 2 cups (200g) broccoli florets
- 2 cloves garlic, minced
- 1 teaspoon ginger, minced

For the sauce:

- ¼ cup (60ml) soy sauce
- 2 tablespoons oyster sauce
- 1 tablespoon cornstarch mixed with 2 tablespoons water

Instructions:

1. Stir-fry beef until browned, then remove.
2. Sauté garlic and ginger, then add broccoli and sauce.
3. Stir in beef and cornstarch slurry, then cook until thickened.

Pepper Steak

Ingredients:

- 1 lb (450g) flank steak, sliced thinly
- 1 red bell pepper, sliced
- 1 green bell pepper, sliced
- 2 cloves garlic, minced
- 1 teaspoon ginger, minced

For the sauce:

- ¼ cup (60ml) soy sauce
- 1 tablespoon oyster sauce
- 1 teaspoon cornstarch mixed with 2 tablespoons water

Instructions:

1. Stir-fry beef until browned, then remove.
2. Sauté garlic, ginger, and bell peppers.
3. Add sauce and beef, cooking until thickened.

Honey Walnut Shrimp

Ingredients:

- 1 lb (450g) shrimp, peeled
- ½ cup (65g) cornstarch
- Oil for frying

For the sauce:

- ¼ cup (60ml) mayonnaise
- 2 tablespoons honey
- 1 tablespoon sweetened condensed milk
- ½ cup (60g) candied walnuts

Instructions:

1. Coat shrimp in cornstarch and fry until crispy.
2. Mix sauce ingredients and toss shrimp.
3. Garnish with candied walnuts.

Salt and Pepper Shrimp

Ingredients:

- 1 lb (450g) shrimp, shell on
- ½ cup (65g) cornstarch
- 1 teaspoon salt
- 1 teaspoon black pepper
- 1 red chili, chopped

Instructions:

1. Coat shrimp in cornstarch and fry until crispy.
2. Sauté chili, then toss shrimp with salt and pepper.

Szechuan Shrimp

Ingredients:

- 1 lb (450g) shrimp, peeled
- 1 teaspoon ginger, minced
- 2 cloves garlic, minced
- 2 dried red chilies, chopped

For the sauce:

- 2 tablespoons soy sauce
- 1 tablespoon rice vinegar
- 1 tablespoon sugar
- 1 teaspoon cornstarch mixed with 2 tablespoons water

Instructions:

1. Stir-fry shrimp, then remove.
2. Sauté chilies, garlic, and ginger.
3. Add shrimp and sauce, cook until thickened.

Hot and Sour Soup

Ingredients:

- 4 cups (1L) chicken broth
- ½ cup (120ml) soy sauce
- ¼ cup (60ml) rice vinegar
- 1 teaspoon white pepper
- 1 teaspoon cornstarch mixed with 2 tablespoons water
- ½ cup (75g) mushrooms, sliced
- ½ cup (75g) tofu, cubed
- 1 egg, beaten
- 1 green onion, sliced

Instructions:

1. Bring broth to a boil, add soy sauce, vinegar, and white pepper.
2. Add mushrooms and tofu, simmer for 5 minutes.
3. Stir in cornstarch slurry until thickened.
4. Slowly drizzle in the egg while stirring.
5. Garnish with green onions.

Egg Drop Soup

Ingredients:

- 4 cups (1L) chicken broth
- ½ teaspoon ginger, minced
- 1 teaspoon cornstarch mixed with 2 tablespoons water
- 2 eggs, beaten
- 1 green onion, sliced

Instructions:

1. Bring broth to a simmer, add ginger.
2. Stir in cornstarch slurry until slightly thickened.
3. Slowly drizzle in eggs while stirring.
4. Garnish with green onions.

Wonton Soup

Ingredients:

For the wontons:

- ½ lb (225g) ground pork
- 1 teaspoon soy sauce
- 1 teaspoon sesame oil
- ½ teaspoon ginger, minced
- 1 green onion, chopped
- 20 wonton wrappers

For the soup:

- 4 cups (1L) chicken broth
- 1 teaspoon soy sauce
- 1 teaspoon sesame oil

Instructions:

1. Mix pork, soy sauce, sesame oil, ginger, and green onion.
2. Place filling in wonton wrappers, seal with water, and fold.
3. Boil broth, add soy sauce and sesame oil.
4. Drop wontons in broth, cook for 3-4 minutes.

Chicken Lo Mein

Ingredients:

- 8 oz (225g) lo mein noodles
- 1 cup (150g) shredded chicken
- ½ cup (75g) bell peppers, sliced
- ½ cup (75g) carrots, julienned
- 2 cloves garlic, minced

For the sauce:

- ¼ cup (60ml) soy sauce
- 1 tablespoon oyster sauce
- 1 teaspoon sesame oil
- 1 teaspoon cornstarch mixed with 2 tablespoons water

Instructions:

1. Cook noodles and set aside.
2. Stir-fry chicken, garlic, and vegetables.
3. Add sauce and noodles, tossing until combined.

Beef Lo Mein

Ingredients:

- 8 oz (225g) lo mein noodles
- 1 cup (150g) beef, thinly sliced
- ½ cup (75g) mushrooms, sliced
- ½ cup (75g) cabbage, shredded
- 2 cloves garlic, minced

For the sauce:

- ¼ cup (60ml) soy sauce
- 1 tablespoon oyster sauce
- 1 teaspoon sesame oil
- 1 teaspoon cornstarch mixed with 2 tablespoons water

Instructions:

1. Cook noodles and set aside.
2. Stir-fry beef, garlic, and vegetables.
3. Add sauce and noodles, tossing until combined.

Shrimp Lo Mein

Ingredients:

- 8 oz (225g) lo mein noodles
- 1 cup (150g) shrimp, peeled
- ½ cup (75g) bell peppers, sliced
- ½ cup (75g) snap peas
- 2 cloves garlic, minced

For the sauce:

- ¼ cup (60ml) soy sauce
- 1 tablespoon oyster sauce
- 1 teaspoon sesame oil
- 1 teaspoon cornstarch mixed with 2 tablespoons water

Instructions:

1. Cook noodles and set aside.
2. Stir-fry shrimp, garlic, and vegetables.
3. Add sauce and noodles, tossing until combined.

Chicken Chow Mein

Ingredients:

- 8 oz (225g) chow mein noodles
- 1 cup (150g) shredded chicken
- ½ cup (75g) bean sprouts
- ½ cup (75g) shredded cabbage
- 2 cloves garlic, minced

For the sauce:

- ¼ cup (60ml) soy sauce
- 1 tablespoon oyster sauce
- 1 teaspoon sesame oil

Instructions:

1. Cook noodles and set aside.
2. Stir-fry chicken, garlic, and vegetables.
3. Add sauce and noodles, tossing until combined.

Beef Chow Fun

Ingredients:

- 8 oz (225g) wide rice noodles
- 1 cup (150g) beef, thinly sliced
- ½ cup (75g) bean sprouts
- ½ cup (75g) green onions, sliced
- 2 cloves garlic, minced

For the sauce:

- ¼ cup (60ml) soy sauce
- 1 tablespoon oyster sauce
- 1 teaspoon sesame oil

Instructions:

1. Cook noodles and set aside.
2. Stir-fry beef, garlic, and vegetables.
3. Add sauce and noodles, tossing until combined.

Shrimp Fried Rice

Ingredients:

- 2 cups (400g) cooked rice
- 1 cup (150g) shrimp, peeled
- ½ cup (75g) peas and carrots
- 2 eggs, beaten
- 2 cloves garlic, minced

For the sauce:

- 2 tablespoons soy sauce
- 1 teaspoon sesame oil

Instructions:

1. Stir-fry shrimp and garlic.
2. Push to the side, scramble eggs in the pan.
3. Add rice, vegetables, and sauce. Stir-fry until combined.

Chicken Fried Rice

Ingredients:

- 2 cups (400g) cooked rice
- 1 cup (150g) shredded chicken
- ½ cup (75g) peas and carrots
- 2 eggs, beaten
- 2 cloves garlic, minced

For the sauce:

- 2 tablespoons soy sauce
- 1 teaspoon sesame oil

Instructions:

1. Stir-fry chicken and garlic.
2. Push to the side, scramble eggs in the pan.
3. Add rice, vegetables, and sauce. Stir-fry until combined.

Yangzhou Fried Rice (Yangzhou Chao Fan)

Ingredients:

- 2 cups (400g) cooked jasmine rice
- ½ cup (75g) shrimp, peeled and chopped
- ½ cup (75g) cooked diced ham
- ½ cup (75g) peas and carrots
- 2 eggs, beaten
- 2 cloves garlic, minced
- 2 tablespoons soy sauce
- 1 teaspoon sesame oil
- 2 green onions, chopped

Instructions:

1. Stir-fry shrimp and ham with garlic in a pan.
2. Push to the side, scramble eggs.
3. Add rice, peas, carrots, soy sauce, and sesame oil.
4. Stir-fry until combined, garnish with green onions.

Egg Foo Young

Ingredients:

- 4 eggs
- ½ cup (75g) cooked shrimp or chicken
- ½ cup (75g) bean sprouts
- ¼ cup (30g) mushrooms, sliced
- ¼ cup (30g) green onions, chopped
- 1 teaspoon soy sauce

For the sauce:

- ½ cup (120ml) chicken broth
- 1 teaspoon cornstarch mixed with 2 tablespoons water
- 1 teaspoon soy sauce

Instructions:

1. Mix eggs with shrimp/chicken, bean sprouts, mushrooms, green onions, and soy sauce.
2. Cook in a hot pan like pancakes.
3. Heat sauce ingredients in a pot until thickened.
4. Pour sauce over egg patties and serve.

Moo Goo Gai Pan

Ingredients:

- 1 lb (450g) chicken breast, sliced thinly
- 1 cup (150g) mushrooms, sliced
- ½ cup (75g) snow peas
- ½ cup (75g) bamboo shoots
- 1 teaspoon ginger, minced
- 2 cloves garlic, minced

For the sauce:

- ¼ cup (60ml) chicken broth
- 2 tablespoons soy sauce
- 1 teaspoon cornstarch mixed with 2 tablespoons water

Instructions:

1. Stir-fry chicken, then remove.
2. Sauté garlic, ginger, mushrooms, snow peas, and bamboo shoots.
3. Add chicken and sauce, cook until thickened.

Hunan Chicken

Ingredients:

- 1 lb (450g) chicken breast, sliced
- ½ cup (75g) bell peppers, sliced
- ½ cup (75g) carrots, julienned
- 2 cloves garlic, minced
- 1 teaspoon ginger, minced
- 1 teaspoon chili paste

For the sauce:

- 2 tablespoons soy sauce
- 1 tablespoon rice vinegar
- 1 teaspoon cornstarch mixed with 2 tablespoons water

Instructions:

1. Stir-fry chicken until cooked, then remove.
2. Sauté garlic, ginger, bell peppers, and carrots.
3. Add chicken, chili paste, and sauce. Stir until thickened.

Szechuan Chicken

Ingredients:

- 1 lb (450g) chicken, diced
- ½ cup (75g) bell peppers, sliced
- ½ cup (75g) peanuts
- 2 dried red chilies, chopped
- 1 teaspoon Szechuan peppercorns
- 2 cloves garlic, minced
- 1 teaspoon ginger, minced

For the sauce:

- 2 tablespoons soy sauce
- 1 tablespoon rice vinegar
- 1 tablespoon hoisin sauce
- 1 teaspoon cornstarch mixed with 2 tablespoons water

Instructions:

1. Stir-fry chicken, then remove.
2. Sauté garlic, ginger, chilies, and peppercorns.
3. Add chicken, bell peppers, peanuts, and sauce.

Cashew Chicken

Ingredients:

- 1 lb (450g) chicken breast, diced
- ½ cup (75g) cashews
- ½ cup (75g) bell peppers, diced
- ½ cup (75g) mushrooms, sliced
- 2 cloves garlic, minced

For the sauce:

- 2 tablespoons soy sauce
- 1 tablespoon oyster sauce
- 1 teaspoon cornstarch mixed with 2 tablespoons water

Instructions:

1. Stir-fry chicken, then remove.
2. Sauté garlic, bell peppers, and mushrooms.
3. Add chicken, cashews, and sauce. Stir until thickened.

Lemon Chicken

Ingredients:

- 1 lb (450g) boneless chicken, cut into strips
- ½ cup (65g) cornstarch
- 1 egg, beaten
- Oil for frying

For the sauce:

- ½ cup (120ml) chicken broth
- ¼ cup (60ml) lemon juice
- 2 tablespoons sugar
- 1 teaspoon cornstarch mixed with 2 tablespoons water

Instructions:

1. Coat chicken in egg and cornstarch, then fry until crispy.
2. Heat sauce ingredients in a pot until thickened.
3. Toss fried chicken in sauce and serve.

Crispy Duck with Hoisin Sauce

Ingredients:

- 1 whole duck
- 1 tablespoon five-spice powder
- 2 tablespoons soy sauce
- 1 tablespoon honey
- ½ teaspoon salt

For serving:

- Hoisin sauce
- Mandarin pancakes
- Sliced green onions

Instructions:

1. Rub duck with five-spice, soy sauce, honey, and salt.
2. Roast at 375°F (190°C) for 1 ½ hours.
3. Shred duck and serve with hoisin sauce, pancakes, and green onions.

Chinese BBQ Pork (Char Siu)

Ingredients:

- 1 lb (450g) pork tenderloin
- 2 tablespoons hoisin sauce
- 1 tablespoon soy sauce
- 1 tablespoon honey
- 1 teaspoon five-spice powder
- 1 teaspoon garlic, minced

Instructions:

1. Marinate pork in sauce overnight.
2. Roast at 375°F (190°C) for 40 minutes, basting occasionally.

Teriyaki Chicken

Ingredients:

- 1 lb (450g) boneless chicken thighs
- ¼ cup (60ml) soy sauce
- 2 tablespoons honey
- 1 tablespoon rice vinegar
- 1 teaspoon ginger, minced
- 1 teaspoon garlic, minced

Instructions:

1. Marinate chicken in sauce for 30 minutes.
2. Grill or pan-fry until caramelized.

Garlic Green Beans

Ingredients:

- 2 cups (200g) green beans
- 2 cloves garlic, minced
- 1 tablespoon soy sauce
- 1 teaspoon sesame oil

Instructions:

1. Stir-fry green beans until blistered.
2. Add garlic and soy sauce, cook for 2 minutes.

Mapo Tofu

Ingredients:

- 1 block (14 oz) silken tofu, cubed
- ½ lb (225g) ground pork
- 2 tablespoons doubanjiang (fermented chili bean paste)
- 1 teaspoon Sichuan peppercorns, ground
- 2 cloves garlic, minced
- 1 teaspoon ginger, minced
- 1 cup (240ml) chicken broth
- 1 teaspoon soy sauce
- 1 teaspoon cornstarch mixed with 2 tablespoons water
- 2 green onions, chopped

Instructions:

1. Sauté ground pork until browned, then add garlic, ginger, and doubanjiang.
2. Pour in chicken broth, add tofu, and simmer for 5 minutes.
3. Stir in soy sauce, cornstarch slurry, and Sichuan peppercorns.
4. Garnish with green onions and serve.

Salt and Pepper Tofu

Ingredients:

- 1 block (14 oz) firm tofu, cubed
- ½ cup (65g) cornstarch
- 1 teaspoon salt
- 1 teaspoon black pepper
- 1 red chili, chopped
- 2 green onions, chopped
- Oil for frying

Instructions:

1. Coat tofu in cornstarch, then fry until crispy.
2. Sauté chili and green onions, toss with tofu, salt, and pepper.

Steamed Fish with Ginger and Scallions

Ingredients:

- 1 whole fish (or fillets, about 1 lb)
- 2 tablespoons soy sauce
- 1 teaspoon sesame oil
- 2 cloves garlic, minced
- 1-inch piece ginger, julienned
- 2 green onions, julienned

Instructions:

1. Steam fish for 10-12 minutes until cooked.
2. Heat soy sauce, sesame oil, garlic, and ginger in a pan.
3. Pour over fish and garnish with green onions.

Chinese Scallion Pancakes

Ingredients:

- 2 cups (250g) all-purpose flour
- ¾ cup (180ml) warm water
- ½ teaspoon salt
- ¼ cup (30g) chopped scallions
- 2 tablespoons vegetable oil

Instructions:

1. Mix flour, salt, and water into a dough. Rest for 30 minutes.
2. Roll out, sprinkle with scallions, and roll into a spiral. Flatten into a pancake.
3. Pan-fry until golden brown on both sides.

Spring Rolls

Ingredients:

- 12 spring roll wrappers
- 1 cup (150g) shredded cabbage
- ½ cup (75g) carrots, julienned
- ½ cup (75g) cooked shrimp or chicken
- 1 teaspoon soy sauce
- 1 teaspoon sesame oil
- Oil for frying

Instructions:

1. Mix cabbage, carrots, and meat with soy sauce and sesame oil.
2. Fill wrappers, roll, and seal edges.
3. Fry until crispy and golden.

Egg Rolls

Ingredients:

- 12 egg roll wrappers
- 1 cup (150g) shredded cabbage
- ½ cup (75g) carrots, julienned
- ½ cup (75g) ground pork
- 1 teaspoon soy sauce
- 1 teaspoon sesame oil
- Oil for frying

Instructions:

1. Sauté pork, cabbage, and carrots with soy sauce.
2. Fill wrappers, roll, and seal edges.
3. Fry until golden and crispy.

Crab Rangoon

Ingredients:

- 8 oz (225g) cream cheese
- ½ cup (100g) crab meat, chopped
- 1 green onion, chopped
- ½ teaspoon garlic powder
- 20 wonton wrappers
- Oil for frying

Instructions:

1. Mix cream cheese, crab, green onions, and garlic powder.
2. Fill wonton wrappers, fold into triangles, and seal edges.
3. Fry until golden brown.

Dumplings (Jiaozi)

Ingredients:

- 2 cups (250g) all-purpose flour
- ¾ cup (180ml) water

For the filling:

- ½ lb (225g) ground pork
- ½ cup (75g) cabbage, minced
- 1 teaspoon soy sauce
- 1 teaspoon sesame oil
- 1 clove garlic, minced

Instructions:

1. Mix flour and water into a dough, rest for 30 minutes.
2. Roll into circles, fill with meat mixture, and seal edges.
3. Boil, steam, or pan-fry until cooked.

Baozi (Steamed Pork Buns)

Ingredients:

For the dough:

- 3 cups (375g) all-purpose flour
- 1 teaspoon yeast
- 1 tablespoon sugar
- ¾ cup (180ml) warm water

For the filling:

- ½ lb (225g) ground pork
- ½ cup (75g) cabbage, minced
- 1 teaspoon soy sauce
- 1 teaspoon sesame oil

Instructions:

1. Mix dough ingredients, knead, and let rise for 1 hour.
2. Mix filling ingredients.
3. Roll out dough, fill with pork mixture, and shape into buns.
4. Steam for 15 minutes.

Dan Dan Noodles

Ingredients:

- 8 oz (225g) wheat noodles
- ½ lb (225g) ground pork
- 2 tablespoons doubanjiang (chili bean paste)
- 1 teaspoon Sichuan peppercorns
- 2 cloves garlic, minced
- 1 teaspoon ginger, minced

For the sauce:

- ¼ cup (60ml) soy sauce
- 2 tablespoons black vinegar
- 1 teaspoon sesame oil

Instructions:

1. Cook noodles and set aside.
2. Stir-fry pork, doubanjiang, garlic, and Sichuan peppercorns.
3. Mix sauce ingredients, toss with noodles and pork.

Chinese Hot Pot

Ingredients:

- 4 cups (1L) chicken broth
- 2 tablespoons soy sauce
- 1 tablespoon chili paste
- 1 teaspoon Sichuan peppercorns
- ½ lb (225g) sliced beef
- ½ lb (225g) shrimp
- ½ lb (225g) tofu, cubed
- 1 cup (150g) mushrooms
- 1 cup (150g) bok choy

Instructions:

1. Bring broth, soy sauce, chili paste, and peppercorns to a boil.
2. Dip meats, tofu, and vegetables into the hot broth to cook.

Peking Duck

Ingredients:

- 1 whole duck
- 2 tablespoons honey
- 1 tablespoon soy sauce
- 1 teaspoon five-spice powder
- 1 teaspoon salt

For serving:

- Mandarin pancakes
- Hoisin sauce
- Sliced green onions

Instructions:

1. Rub duck with honey, soy sauce, five-spice, and salt.
2. Hang to dry for 6 hours.
3. Roast at 375°F (190°C) for 1 ½ hours.
4. Slice and serve with hoisin sauce, pancakes, and green onions.

Black Bean Chicken

Ingredients:

- 1 lb (450g) boneless chicken, sliced
- 2 tablespoons fermented black beans, rinsed and mashed
- 1 bell pepper, sliced
- 1 onion, sliced
- 2 cloves garlic, minced
- 1 teaspoon ginger, minced

For the sauce:

- 2 tablespoons soy sauce
- 1 tablespoon oyster sauce
- 1 teaspoon cornstarch mixed with 2 tablespoons water

Instructions:

1. Stir-fry chicken until browned, then remove.
2. Sauté garlic, ginger, black beans, onion, and bell pepper.
3. Add chicken and sauce, stir-fry until thickened.

Cumin Lamb Stir-Fry

Ingredients:

- 1 lb (450g) lamb, sliced thinly
- 1 teaspoon cumin seeds
- 1 teaspoon chili flakes
- ½ teaspoon Sichuan peppercorns, ground
- 2 cloves garlic, minced
- 1 teaspoon ginger, minced
- ½ cup (75g) red and green bell peppers, sliced

Instructions:

1. Marinate lamb in soy sauce for 30 minutes.
2. Toast cumin, chili flakes, and peppercorns in a pan.
3. Stir-fry lamb, then add garlic, ginger, and bell peppers.
4. Toss with toasted spices and serve.

Sichuan Dry-Fried Green Beans

Ingredients:

- 2 cups (200g) green beans, trimmed
- ½ lb (225g) ground pork
- 1 teaspoon Sichuan peppercorns
- 2 cloves garlic, minced
- 1 teaspoon ginger, minced
- 1 tablespoon soy sauce
- 1 teaspoon chili paste

Instructions:

1. Dry-fry green beans in a pan until wrinkled, then remove.
2. Stir-fry pork, garlic, ginger, and Sichuan peppercorns.
3. Add soy sauce, chili paste, and green beans, stir-fry until combined.

Hot and Spicy Tofu Stir-Fry

Ingredients:

- 1 block (14 oz) firm tofu, cubed
- 1 teaspoon Sichuan peppercorns, ground
- 1 teaspoon chili paste
- 2 cloves garlic, minced
- 1 teaspoon ginger, minced
- ½ cup (75g) bell peppers, sliced
- 1 tablespoon soy sauce

Instructions:

1. Stir-fry tofu until golden, then remove.
2. Sauté garlic, ginger, Sichuan peppercorns, and chili paste.
3. Add tofu, bell peppers, and soy sauce, stir-fry until combined.

Chinese Donuts (Youtiao)

Ingredients:

- 2 cups (250g) all-purpose flour
- 1 teaspoon baking powder
- ½ teaspoon baking soda
- ½ teaspoon salt
- ½ cup (120ml) warm water
- 1 tablespoon vegetable oil
- Oil for frying

Instructions:

1. Mix flour, baking powder, baking soda, salt, water, and oil into a dough.
2. Rest for 1 hour, then roll into strips and twist pairs together.
3. Fry until golden and crispy.

Red Bean Sesame Balls (Jian Dui)

Ingredients:

- 1 cup (150g) glutinous rice flour
- ½ cup (120ml) water
- ¼ cup (50g) sugar
- ½ cup (100g) red bean paste
- ½ cup (75g) sesame seeds
- Oil for frying

Instructions:

1. Mix rice flour, sugar, and water into a dough.
2. Divide into balls, fill with red bean paste, and seal.
3. Roll in sesame seeds and fry until golden brown.

www.ingramcontent.com/pod-product-compliance
Lightning Source LLC
LaVergne TN
LVHW081333060526
838201LV00055B/2613